D0192929

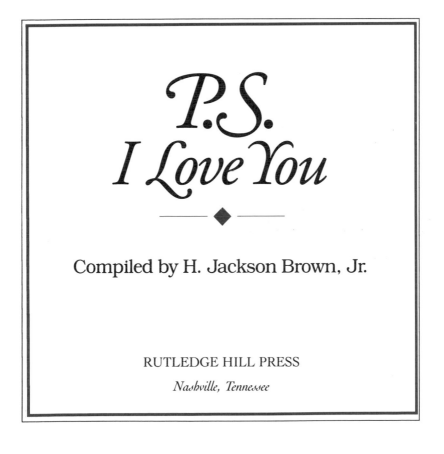

P.S.
I Love You

◆

Compiled by H. Jackson Brown, Jr.

RUTLEDGE HILL PRESS

Nashville, Tennessee

Published in Nashville, Tennessee, by Rutledge Hill Press, Inc., 513 Third Avenue South, Nashville, Tennessee 37210

Library of Congress Cataloging-in-Publication Data

P.S. I love you.

   1. Letter writing—Humor. 2. Mothers—Humor. I. Brown, H. Jackson, 1940–   . II. Title: PS I love you.
PN6231.L44P25   1990   816'.54   90-8309
ISBN 1-55853-071-X

Manufactured in the United States of America

4 5 6 7 8 9 — 95 94 93 92 91

Introduction

Over the years Mom has written my sister and me hundreds of letters. What we cherished most were the little P.S. notes she would write at the end of each one.

There, in just a few words, she would encourage and inspire us with keen observations, gentle humor, and loving advice.

We saved the letters, and this little book is a collection of her P.S. messages that we love the most. Although some were written more than forty years ago, they still ring with truth and insight.

I hope you will enjoy reading them. Perhaps you will be reminded of similar words of wisdom written to you by your mother or father.

As I write this, I am happy to report that Mom is in excellent health and still writing.

I can't wait for her next letter.

H.J.B.

Dedicated to my mother whose love, laughter, encouragement
and values will always guide and inspire me.

Thanks, Mom. I love you.
H. J. B.

P.S.

What you are becoming
is more important than what
you are accomplishing.

I love you,

Mom

P.S.

I know this letter has been
filled with advice — all unsolicited.
Take what you want and
throw the rest away.
As George Bernard Shaw said,

"Advice is like kissing:
it costs nothing and it's a
pleasant thing to do."

I love you,

Mom

P.S.

I love this story about
giving credit where credit is due:

A preacher comes up to a farmer
in his field and remarks, "Mighty
fine farm you and the Lord have made."
"Yep," replies the farmer, "but you should
have seen it when He had it
all to Himself."

I love you,

Mom

P.S.

If there were no one
to watch them drive by,
how many people
would buy a Mercedes?

I love you,

Mom

P.S.

Dearest Daughter,
you don't have to prove yourself
to me, your father, or to anyone.
If you have done your best,
that's all that matters.
Are you content and
satisfied with your efforts?
That's the only question
to ask.

I love you,

Mom

P.S.

Regarding your D in biology,
let me only say that
sometimes a good scare
is worth more than good advice.

I love you,

Mom

P.S.

One of your father's clients sent him a
lovely paperweight with this inscription:

PEOPLE CAN BE DIVIDED INTO THREE GROUPS:
    THOSE WHO MAKE THINGS HAPPEN.
    THOSE WHO WATCH THINGS HAPPEN.
    THOSE WHO WONDER WHAT HAPPENED.
CONGRATULATIONS ON BEING THE CAPTAIN OF
            THE FIRST GROUP.

You have a very special father.

I love you,

Mom

P.S.

You're learning that nothing
worthwhile ever comes without hard work.
As Grandfather Harper used to say,

"To enjoy the cider
you must first peel the apple."

I love you,

Mom

P.S.

Twenty years from now
you will be more disappointed
by the things you didn't do than
by the ones you did do.
So throw off the bowlines.
Sail away from the safe harbor.
Catch the trade winds in your sails.
Explore. Dream. Discover.

I love you,

Mom

P.S.

An older gentleman in front of me at
the check-out at Kroger's was wearing
a hat with this inscription:

IF WE HAD KNOWN
GRANDKIDS WERE SO MUCH FUN,
WE'D HAVE HAD THEM FIRST.

I bet he's a great granddad!

I love you,

Mom

P.S.

As they say in Texas,

If you've done it,
It ain't braggin'.

I love you,

Mom

P.S.

Life is teaching you
some painful lessons.
But it is from adversity
that strength is born.
You may have lost the inning,
but I know you'll
win the game.

I love you,

Mom

P.S.

Your father defines an honest man
as someone you could play checkers with
over the telephone.

I love you,

Mom

P.S.

Luck may bring you riches,
but it will never bring you wisdom.

I love you,

Mom

P.S.

Instead of waiting for
someone to bring you flowers,
why not plant your own garden?

I love you,

Mom

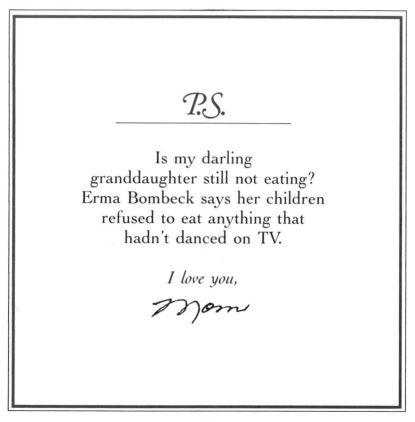

P.S.

Is my darling
granddaughter still not eating?
Erma Bombeck says her children
refused to eat anything that
hadn't danced on TV.

I love you,

Mom

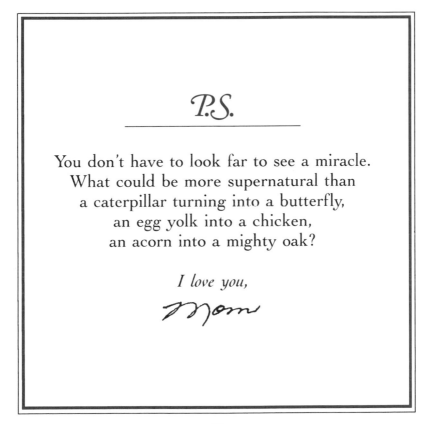

P.S.

You don't have to look far to see a miracle.
What could be more supernatural than
a caterpillar turning into a butterfly,
an egg yolk into a chicken,
an acorn into a mighty oak?

I love you,

Mom

P.S.

Last week
I met a young salesman
in a shoe store wearing a
button with this saying:

IF YOU DON'T HAVE A SMILE,
I'LL GIVE YOU ONE OF MINE.

He'd made it himself.
I love it!

I love you,

Mom

P.S.

The greatest accomplishments in
science and the arts have been made
by individuals acting alone.
No park has a statue dedicated
to a committee.

I love you,

Mom

P.S.

You'll never
build a reputation,
a business, or a relationship
on what you *intend* to do.
Your intentions may be honorable
and sincere, but unless you
put them into action,
nothing is changed.

I love you,

Mom

P.S.

No failure
is ever final — nor
is any success.

I love you,

Mom

P.S.

When you invite trouble,
it's usually quick to accept.

I love you,

Mom

P.S.

Awareness is a major key to success.
Keep your radar finely tuned.
You never know where
a good idea will come from
or how far it will take you.

I love you,

Mom

P.S.

Not that you asked, but here's
my advice on financial matters:

Live slightly beneath your means.

As Shakespeare's King Lear advised,
"Have more than thou showest."

I love you,

Mom

P.S.

Promise only what you can deliver.
Then deliver *more* than you promise.

I love you,

Mom

P.S.

Carrying a grudge is like a run
in a stocking — it can only get worse.
Forgiveness is the answer.

I love you,

Mom

P.S.

Dale Carnegie wrote this
almost fifty years ago.
It's as true today as it was then:

"You can make more friends
in two months by becoming
genuinely interested in other people
than you can in two years
by trying to get other people
interested in you."

I love you,

Mom

P.S.

Your father says
success in business
is like riding a bicycle.
Either you keep moving
or you fall over.

Keep it moving!

I love you,

Mom

P.S.

The only thing that
ever sat its way to success
was a hen.

I love you,

Mom

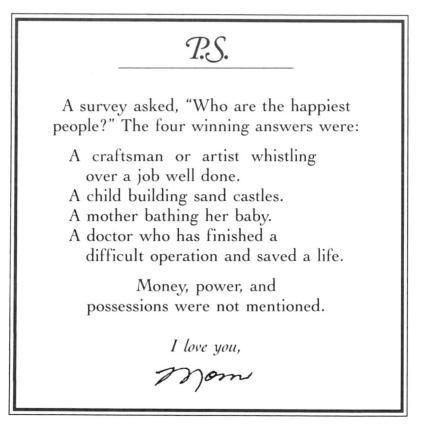

P.S.

A survey asked, "Who are the happiest people?" The four winning answers were:

A craftsman or artist whistling over a job well done.
A child building sand castles.
A mother bathing her baby.
A doctor who has finished a difficult operation and saved a life.

Money, power, and possessions were not mentioned.

I love you,

Mom

P.S.

A person who is always
telling you how honest he is
probably has his own suspicions.

I love you,

Mom

P.S.

I know things are tough right now.
Life sometimes gives you the test before
you've had a chance to study the lesson.

I know you'll succeed. Keep on
keeping on.

I love you,

Mom

P.S.

Sometimes the heart sees
what is invisible to the eye.

I love you,

Mom

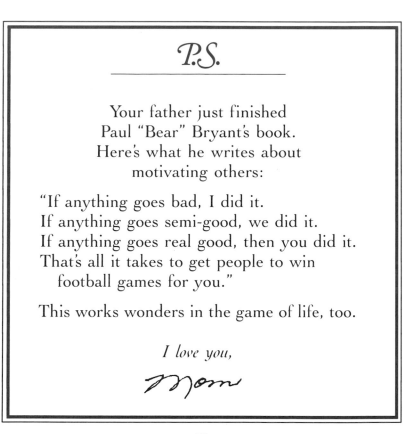

P.S.

Your father just finished
Paul "Bear" Bryant's book.
Here's what he writes about
motivating others:

"If anything goes bad, I did it.
If anything goes semi-good, we did it.
If anything goes real good, then you did it.
That's all it takes to get people to win
    football games for you."

This works wonders in the game of life, too.

I love you,

Mom

P.S.

I have to admit that after helping
your father rake all the leaves Saturday,
I'm beginning to feel my age.
But you won't hear me
complain about getting older.
Just think of the people
who are denied the privilege.

I love you,

Mom

P.S.

I saw a sign with the word *FIDO* on the
back of a Winnebago at a filling station.
I asked the driver if it was
the name of his dog.
"Oh no," he replied.
"It's to remind me that when
someone is discourteous on the road
I should just Forget It and Drive On."

Good advice.

I love you,

Mom

P.S.

Praise is satisfying to receive,
but it never teaches you anything new.

I love you,

Mom

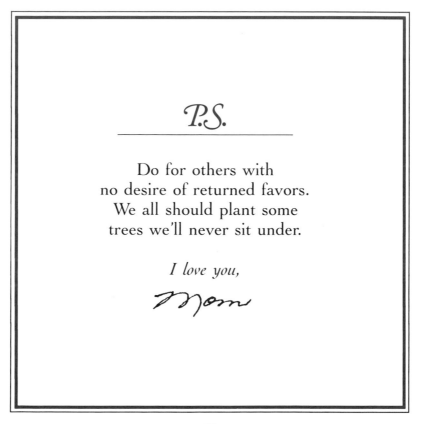

P.S.

Do for others with
no desire of returned favors.
We all should plant some
trees we'll never sit under.

I love you,

Mom

P.S.

If you know people who
try to drown their sorrows,
you might tell them
sorrows know how to swim.

I love you,

Mom

P.S.

Someone asked me last week what I did.
I thought for a moment
and answered, "Explorer."
I was pleased with my reply.

I love you,

Mom

P.S.

Don't be afraid to go out on a limb.
That's where the fruit is.

I love you,

Mom

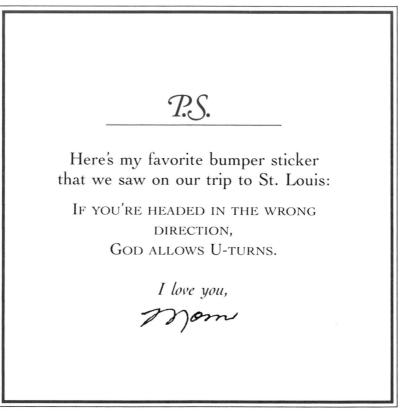

P.S.

Here's my favorite bumper sticker
that we saw on our trip to St. Louis:

IF YOU'RE HEADED IN THE WRONG
DIRECTION,
GOD ALLOWS U-TURNS.

I love you,

Mom

P.S.

Now that you and your sister are graduated, happily married, and working at jobs that are challenging and financially rewarding, your father and I feel it's finally our time. Someone said, "Life doesn't begin at conception, nor at birth, but when the kids leave home and the dog dies." We eagerly await the next chapter in our lives. Wagons ho!

I love you,

Mom

P.S.

Aunt Bessie says one of
the best things about getting older
is that all those things you wanted
and couldn't afford when
you were younger,
you no longer want.

I love you,

Mom

P.S.

The great man shows his greatness
by the way he treats the little man.

I love you,

Mom

P.S.

Luck is like a chameleon.
Give it a little time
and it will surely change.

I love you,

Mom

P.S.

People often admit to
a bad memory — but never
to bad judgment.

I love you,

Mom

P.S.

When you are angry or
frustrated, what comes out?
Whatever it is, it's a good
indication of what
you're made of.

I love you,

Mom

P.S.

I've just finished reading the book
The 100 Most Influential Persons in History.
I am struck by the one thing I have in
common with all of them — time.
These men and women
who changed the world did not have any
more hours a day than you and I.
I'm convinced judicious use of time is one of
the major contributors to success.

I love you,

Mom

P.S.

Your Aunt Louise has stopped smoking,
no ifs, ands, or butts about it.

I love you,

Mom

P.S.

True wealth is what you are,
not what you have.

I love you,

Mom

P.S.

We seldom enjoy leisure
we haven't earned.

I love you,

Mom

P.S.

If at the end of a day
you feel dog-tired,
maybe it's because
you growled all day.

I love you,

Mom

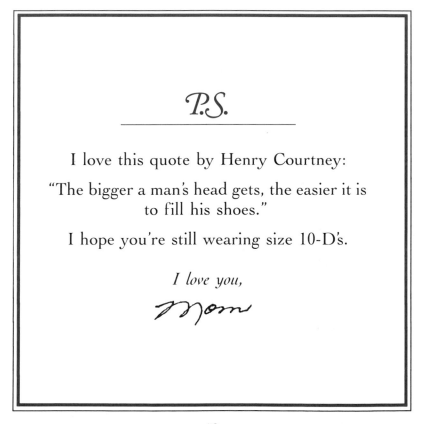

P.S.

I love this quote by Henry Courtney:

"The bigger a man's head gets, the easier it is to fill his shoes."

I hope you're still wearing size 10-D's.

I love you,

Mom

P.S.

You can consider yourself
a good manager when
you get superior work
from average people.

I love you,

Mom

P.S.

You master your enemies
not by force
but by forgiveness.

I love you,

Mom

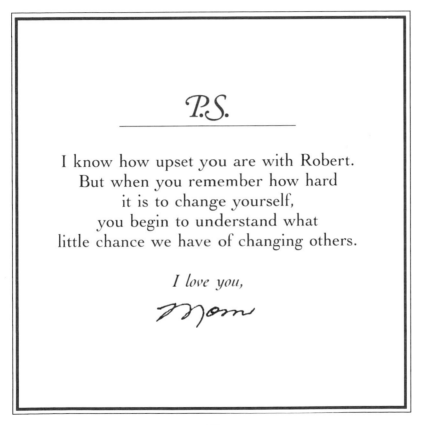

P.S.

I know how upset you are with Robert.
But when you remember how hard
it is to change yourself,
you begin to understand what
little chance we have of changing others.

I love you,

Mom

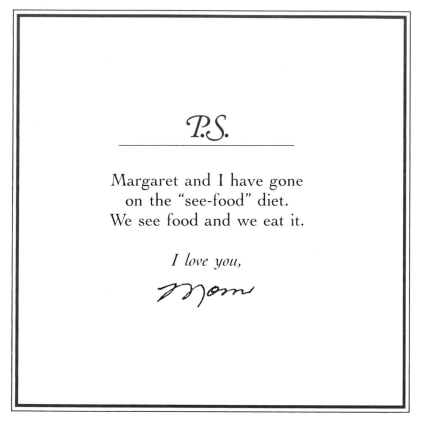

P.S.

Margaret and I have gone
on the "see-food" diet.
We see food and we eat it.

I love you,

Mom

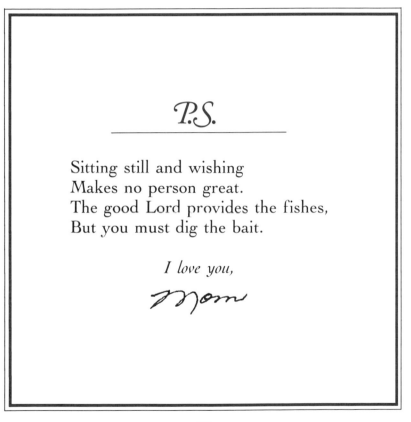

P.S.

Sitting still and wishing
Makes no person great.
The good Lord provides the fishes,
But you must dig the bait.

I love you,

Mom

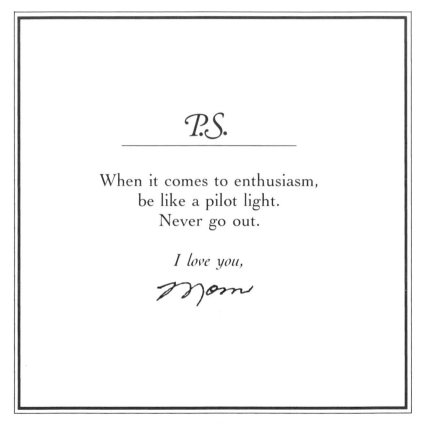

P.S.

When it comes to enthusiasm,
be like a pilot light.
Never go out.

I love you,

Mom

P.S.

Old Chinese proverb:

He who goes out of his house
in search of happiness
runs after a shadow.

I love you,

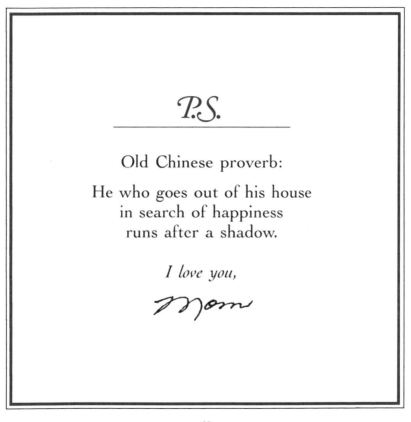

P.S.

Good manners sometimes
means simply putting up with
other people's bad manners.

I love you,

Mom

P.S.

If you keep waiting
for just the right time,
you may never begin.
Begin now!
Begin where you are
with what you are.

I love you,

Mom

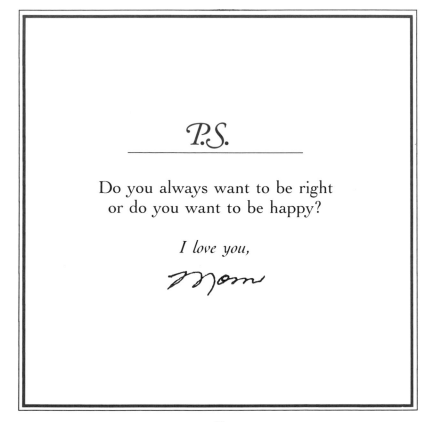

P.S.

Do you always want to be right
or do you want to be happy?

I love you,

Mom

P.S.

Sorry to hear about your first confrontation with a customer. Here's a response that's always worked for me. The next time you face a customer who has every right to be upset say something like this:

"I don't blame you for feeling as you do. If I were you, I'd feel exactly the same way. What would you like for me to do?"

These are magical, healing words and you'll be surprised at how reasonable people become when they feel you are on their side.

I love you,

Mom

P.S.

Regarding the contract
with your publisher,
read it carefully.
Remember, the big print giveth
and the small print taketh away.

I love you,

Mom

P.S.

It is my observation
that too many of us are
spending money we haven't earned
to buy things we don't need
to impress people we don't like.

I love you,

Mom

P.S.

For Julie's fortieth birthday,
someone gave her an enormous card
with this inscription:

WHEN YOU'RE OVER THE HILL,
YOU PICK UP SPEED.

Your father and I are really cruisin'!

I love you,

Mom

P.S.

There's trouble at your father's office.
An employee is suing.
Your father says you enter a lawsuit a pig
and come out a sausage.

Oink.

I love you,

Mom

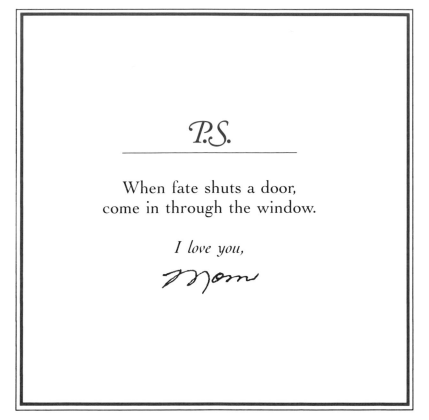

P.S.

When fate shuts a door,
come in through the window.

I love you,

Mom

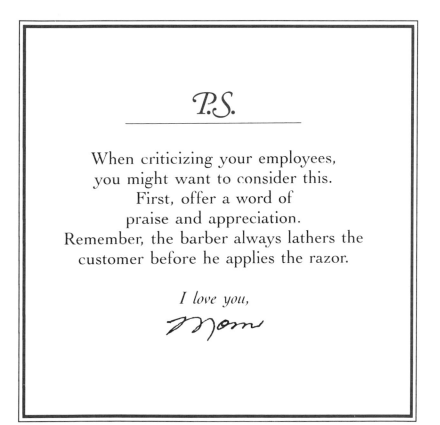

P.S.

When criticizing your employees,
you might want to consider this.
First, offer a word of
praise and appreciation.
Remember, the barber always lathers the
customer before he applies the razor.

I love you,

Mom

P.S.

The most important thing
a father can do for his children
is to love their mother.

Your father does such a good job of that.

I love you,

Mom

P.S.

Everyone you meet knows
something you don't know
but need to know.
Learn from them.

I love you,

Mom

P.S.

A recent study revealed that
people who did volunteer work
at least once a week
outlived those who did none,
two-and-a-half to one.
That implies that doing something
for other people is a powerful contributor
to health and long life.

I love you,

Mom

P.S.

Did you hear the story about
the optimist and the pessimist?
The optimist goes to the window every
morning and says, "Good morning, God."
The pessimist goes to the window
and says, "Good God, morning."

I've always loved your optimism.

I love you,

Mom

P.S.

Your father says inflation
hasn't ruined everything.
A dime can still be used
as a screwdriver.

I love you,

Mom

P.S.

A friend is a person who
knows all about you but
likes you anyway.

I love you,

Mom

P.S.

Elizabeth calls life's disappointments
"speed bumps"—things you have
to get over in order to enjoy
the rest of life's journey.

I love you,

Mom

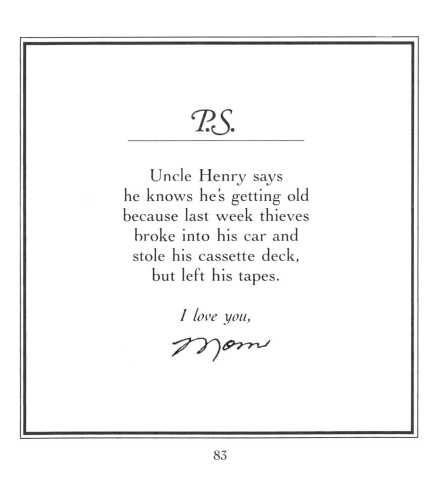

P.S.

Uncle Henry says
he knows he's getting old
because last week thieves
broke into his car and
stole his cassette deck,
but left his tapes.

I love you,

Mom

P.S.

When examining your marriage,
use a telescope — only look
through the wrong end.

I love you,

Mom

P.S.

You'll learn more
about a road by traveling it
than by consulting all the
maps in the world.

I love you,

Mom

P.S.

I know you are angry with me.
But don't forget for a second
that I love you. No matter what
you do, or say, or think,
you can always depend on
my support and love.

I love you,

Mom

P.S.

I've never seen a smiling face
that was not beautiful.

I love you,

Mom

P.S.

To change everything,
simply change your attitude.

I love you,

Mom

P.S.

I love your laughter.
And I love how you
make me laugh.

I love you,

Mom

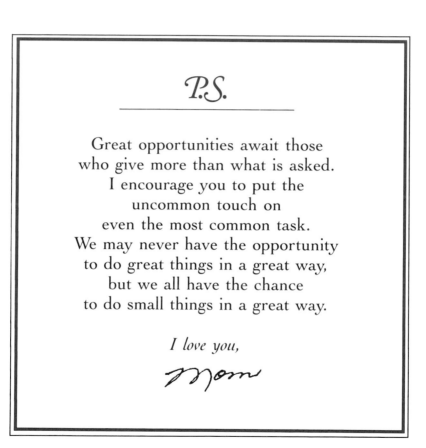

P.S.

Great opportunities await those
who give more than what is asked.
I encourage you to put the
uncommon touch on
even the most common task.
We may never have the opportunity
to do great things in a great way,
but we all have the chance
to do small things in a great way.

I love you,

Mom

P.S.

To be bitter
is to waste precious
moments of a life that's
too short already.

I love you,

Mom

P.S.

Today, give a stranger
one of your smiles.
It might be the only sunshine
he sees all day.

I love you,

Mom

P.S.

Do you want credit or results?
This quote hangs in the office
of the president of Neiman-Marcus:

THERE'S NO LIMIT TO WHAT YOU CAN ACHIEVE
IF YOU DON'T MIND WHO GETS THE CREDIT.

I love you,

Mom

P.S.

A business executive once told
his associates:

"Reach for the stars.
You might not get them,
but you won't wind up with
a handful of mud either."

I love you,

Mom

P.S.

This week I've been trying to think
before I speak — to say something
positive and kind or nothing at all.
Winston Churchill said:

"By swallowing evil words unsaid,
no one has ever harmed his stomach."

I love you,

Mom

P.S.

To get more out of life,
give more of yourself.

I love you,

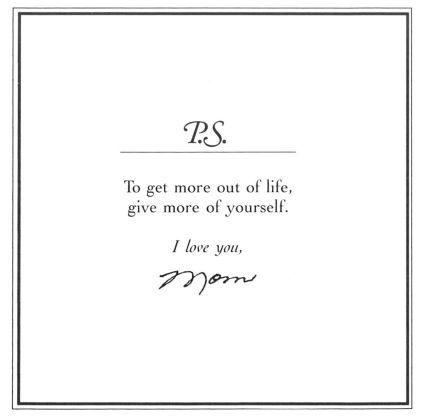

_P.S._

If you're headed in the right direction,
each step, no matter how small,
is getting you closer to your goal.

I love you,

Mom

P.S.

Go for it! Take a chance.
There are times you must trust
that silent voice inside you.
The experts don't always have
the right answers.

According to the laws of aerodynamics
the bumble bee cannot fly.
I guess no one bothered to tell the bee.

Keep flying!

I love you,

Mom

P.S.

Those who spend most of their time
making and hoarding money
often find the things they want most
cannot be bought.

I love you,

Mom

P.S.

Dreams come true
for those who work
while they dream.

Sweet dreams.

I love you,

Mom

P.S.

In an interview,
the actor Michael Caine told
how his mother encouraged him to be
like a duck — calm on the surface
but always paddling like the
dickens underneath.

I love you,

Mom

P.S.

Only God is in a position
to look down on anyone.

I love you,

Mom

P.S.

Congratulations on your summer job.
As a new sales associate,
just remember that
true salesmanship begins
when the customer says "no."

I love you,

Mom

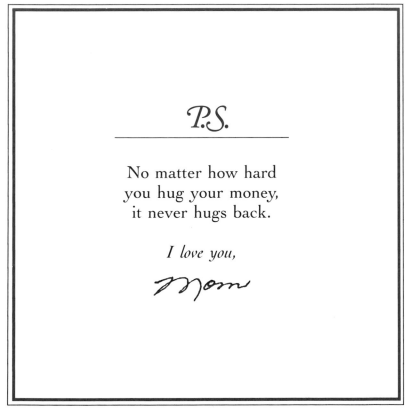

P.S.
___

No matter how hard
you hug your money,
it never hugs back.

I love you,

Mom

P.S.

No one is guaranteed happiness.
Life just gives each
person time and space.
It's up to us to fill it with joy.

I love you,

Mom

P.S.

Your religion is what
you do when the sermon is over.

I love you,

Mom

P.S.

Job security
is being worth more
than you're getting paid.

I love you,

Mom

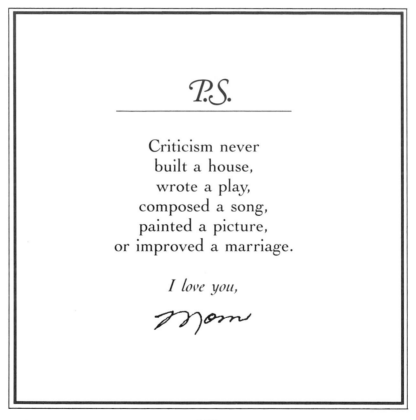

P.S.

Criticism never
built a house,
wrote a play,
composed a song,
painted a picture,
or improved a marriage.

I love you,

Mom

P.S.

I've had this quote from Louise Leber
on the refrigerator all week:

THERE'S ALWAYS ROOM FOR IMPROVEMENT.
IT'S THE BIGGEST ROOM IN THE HOUSE.

I love you,

Mom

P.S.

Middle age is
when you have two choices
and you choose the one
that gets you home earlier.

I love you,

Mom

P.S.

Lyndon Johnson once said that
when anyone tells you
he's just a dumb old country boy,
put your hand on your wallet.

I love you,

Mom

P.S.

The next time someone hurts you
and your first response is to
hurt them back, remember:

The person who pursues revenge
should dig two graves.

I love you,

Mom

P.S.

A trainee has this sign on
his desk at your father's business:

YOU EITHER MAKE DUST
OR YOU EAT DUST.

This is a young man to watch.

I love you,

Mom

P.S.

I'm so glad you and your roommate
enjoyed the brownies.
As some English bard used to say:

"No man can be wise
on an empty stomach."

I love you,

Mom

P.S.

Almost all of our unhappiness
is the result of comparing
ourselves to others.

I love you,

Mom

P.S.

Someone wrote:

"A spade and a kind word
should never be allowed to rust."

That reminds me
of your grandfather's advice
to compliment at least three
people every day.

I love you,

Mom

P.S.

Sometimes your father has
a tendency to boast just a little bit —
especially around old friends.
I left this note in his sock drawer:

Don't brag.
It's not the whistle
that moves the train.

Think he got the message?

I love you,

Mom

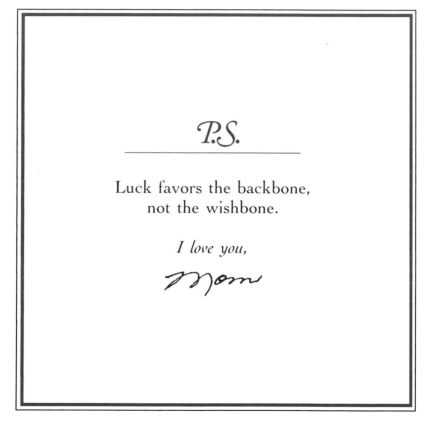

_P.S._

Luck favors the backbone,
not the wishbone.

I love you,

Mom

P.S.

Honey, I know you're disappointed.
We don't always get everything we want.
But to balance that, think of
all the things we don't get
that we don't want.

I love you,

Mom

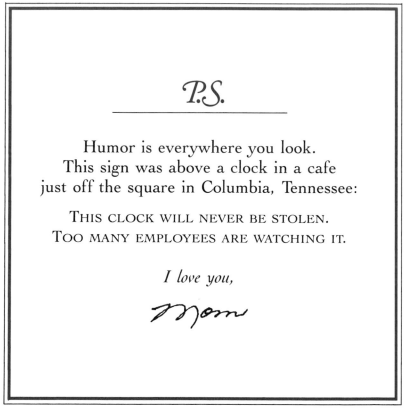

P.S.

Humor is everywhere you look.
This sign was above a clock in a cafe
just off the square in Columbia, Tennessee:

THIS CLOCK WILL NEVER BE STOLEN.
TOO MANY EMPLOYEES ARE WATCHING IT.

I love you,

Mom

P.S.

Every day we are given stones.
But what do we build?
Is it a bridge or is it a wall?

I love you,

Mom

P.S.

I love this quote by Albert Schweitzer:

"Happiness is nothing more than
health and a poor memory."

I love you,

Mom

P.S.

You wouldn't be worried about
what people think of you
if you knew how seldom
they actually do.

I love you,

Mom

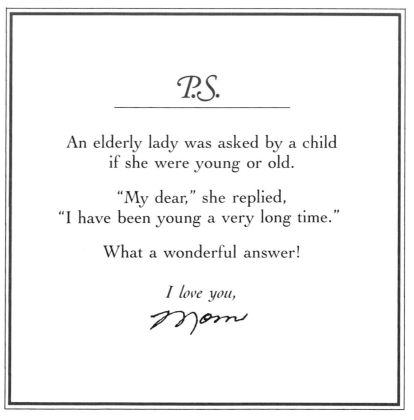

P.S.

An elderly lady was asked by a child
if she were young or old.

"My dear," she replied,
"I have been young a very long time."

What a wonderful answer!

I love you,

Mom

P.S.

Our character is what we do
when we think no one is looking.

I love you,

Mom

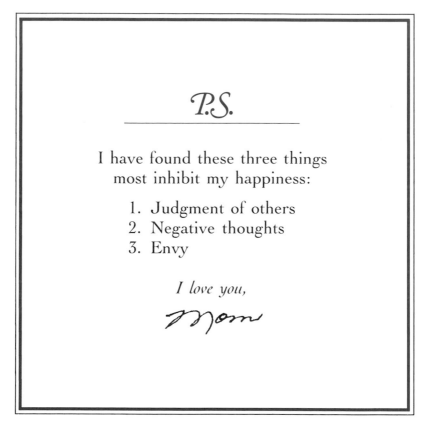

P.S.

I have found these three things
most inhibit my happiness:

1. Judgment of others
2. Negative thoughts
3. Envy

I love you,

Mom

P.S.

Nothing worthwhile
is ever learned
in ten easy lessons.

I love you,

Mom

P.S.

Knowledge without action
is like snow on a hot stove.

I love you,

Mom

P.S.

As you climb the ladder of success,
be sure it's leaning
against the right building.

I love you,

Mom

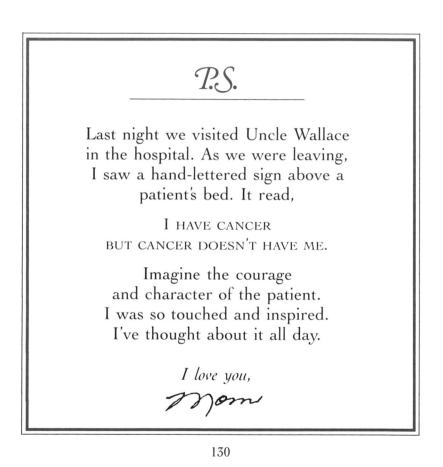

P.S.

Last night we visited Uncle Wallace
in the hospital. As we were leaving,
I saw a hand-lettered sign above a
patient's bed. It read,

I HAVE CANCER
BUT CANCER DOESN'T HAVE ME.

Imagine the courage
and character of the patient.
I was so touched and inspired.
I've thought about it all day.

I love you,

Mom

P.S.

John Luther wrote this about character:

"Good character is more to be praised
than outstanding talent.
Most talents are, to some extent, a gift.
Good character, by contrast, is not
given to us. We have to build it
piece by piece — by thought, choice,
courage, and determination."

I'm so proud of your fine character.

I love you,

Mom

P.S.

A robin is building a nest in
the dogwood tree next to
our kitchen window.
She builds it with such completeness,
such perfection, and with such confidence.
Where does that kind of knowledge
come from?

I love you,

Mom

P.S.

Luck is what happens when
preparation meets opportunity.

I love you,

Mom

P.S.

I hear you have a new heartthrob.
Keep a clear head.
Remember, a person in love
sometimes mistakes a pimple
for a dimple.

I love you,

Mom

P.S.

I couldn't help but smile
when I saw this bumper sticker
on the back of an old pickup truck
parked at Wal-Mart:

MY WIFE TOOK EVERYTHING
BUT THE BLAME.

I love you,

Mom

P.S.

When you have nothing important
or interesting to say,
don't let anyone
persuade you to say it.

I love you,

Mom

$\mathcal{P.S.}$

You are blessed
with many wonderful friends.
But remember,
friends are like house plants.
They require regular care.

I love you,

Mom

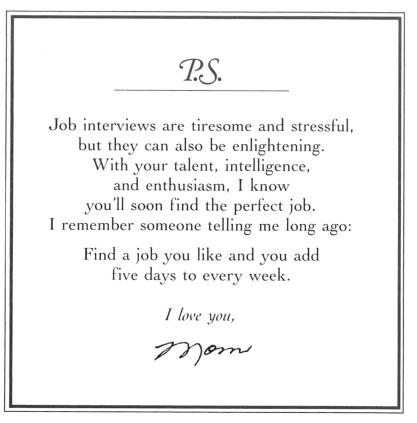

P.S.

Job interviews are tiresome and stressful,
but they can also be enlightening.
With your talent, intelligence,
and enthusiasm, I know
you'll soon find the perfect job.
I remember someone telling me long ago:

Find a job you like and you add
five days to every week.

I love you,

Mom

P.S.

Your father overheard
a farmer at the livestock show
describe his financial condition
in a colorful way:

"I'm as broke
as the Ten Commandments."

I love you,

Mom

P.S.

Margaret has this framed
and hanging in her kitchen:

YOU HAVE TWO CHOICES FOR DINNER.
TAKE IT OR LEAVE IT.

Bon appetit!

I love you,

Mom

P.S.

You will never face
a problem that's not charged
with opportunity.

I love you,

Mom

P.S.

Millions of words
have been written about success.
These by Elbert Hubbard are
among my favorites:

"He has achieved success
who has worked well,
laughed often, and loved much."

I love you,

Mom

P.S.

I know you have an impressive wardrobe.
But of all the things you wear,
your expression is the most important.
If someone remembers your suit
and not your smile,
you didn't smile enough.

I love you,

Mom

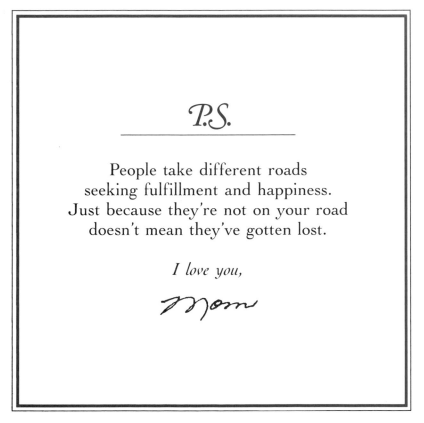

P.S.

People take different roads
seeking fulfillment and happiness.
Just because they're not on your road
doesn't mean they've gotten lost.

I love you,

Mom

P.S.

Last night your father and I
reviewed our retirement savings.
We've decided we have enough
to last us the rest of our lives —
unless we decide to buy something!

Oh, well.

I love you,

Mom

P.S.

Everyone from time to time
needs a little boost.
If you see a turtle on a fence post,
remember he had some help
getting there.

I love you,

Mom

P.S.

The surest way to make yourself happy
is to make someone else happy.

I love you,

Mom

P.S.

One of God's greatest miracles
is to enable ordinary people
to do extraordinary things.

I love you,

Mom

P.S.

If you're doing your best,
you won't have any time
to worry about failure.

I love you,

Mom

P.S.

We can't do much about our appearance,
but we have total control over
the kind of person we become.

I love you,

Mom

P.S.

I know you're angry with Alec.
Why not try this. Write him a letter.
Pour out all of your feelings —
describe your anger and disappointment.
Don't hold anything back.
Then put the letter in a drawer.
After two days take it out and read it.
Do you still want to send it?
I've found that anger and pie crusts
soften after two days.

I love you,

Mom

P.S.

As you begin a new task or assignment,
it is your attitude
more than anything else
that will determine your success.

I love you,

Mom

P.S.

Growing older
can be a wonderful adventure
if you remember that
the important word is *growing*.

I love you,

Mom

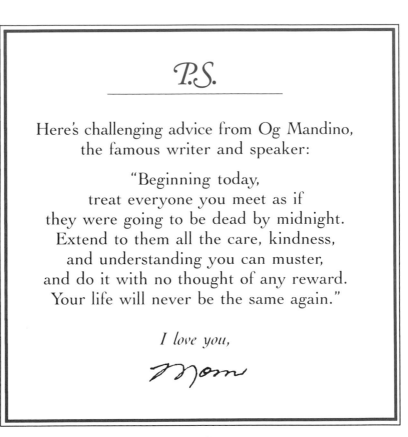

P.S.

Here's challenging advice from Og Mandino,
the famous writer and speaker:

"Beginning today,
treat everyone you meet as if
they were going to be dead by midnight.
Extend to them all the care, kindness,
and understanding you can muster,
and do it with no thought of any reward.
Your life will never be the same again."

I love you,

Mom

P.S.

So you wish that
all the problems at work would go away.
Maybe you'd better think again.
When problems cease, so do opportunities.
Solving problems was the reason
you were hired.
And it's been my experience that
jobs with few problems
don't pay very much.

I love you,

Mom

P.S.

While earning your daily bread,
be sure you share a slice
with those less fortunate.

I love you,

Mom

P.S.

Be smarter than other people —
just don't tell them so.

I love you,

Mom

P.S.

Love is like wildflowers.
It's often found
in the most unlikely places.

I love you,

Mom

P.S.

Remember the Golden Rule.
And remember it's your turn.

I love you,

Mom

P.S.

I don't know the author of the following,
but it is inspiring:

"The people on our planet are not standing
in a line single file. Look closely.
Everyone is really standing in a circle,
holding hands. Whatever you give
to the person standing next to you,
it eventually comes back to you."

Beautiful.

I love you,

Mom